T0158861

THE BIBLICAL ANSWER

ROBERT HUNT

Illustrations by Keil Alderson

WESTBOW
PRESS®
A DIVISION OF THOMAS NELSON
& ZONDERVAN

WestBow Press books may be ordered through booksellers or by contacting:

WestBow Press
A Division of Thomas Nelson & Zondervan
1663 Liberty Drive
Bloomington, IN 47403
www.westbowpress.com
1 (866) 928-1240

ISBN: 978-1-5127-7483-2 (sc)
ISBN: 978-1-5127-7482-5 (e)

Library of Congress Control Number: 2017901834

Print information available on the last page.

WestBow Press rev. date: 04/20/2017

To those who appreciate all of heaven's treasures.

Contents

Preface

The material in this study began as a Sunday evening Bible study for my parishioners. I am indebted to participants in that study for their encouragement to put it in this form. I am also grateful to Nancy L. Sanders for her editorial assistance and for her valuable suggestions, to Bonnie Annis for secretarial help, and to Keil Alderson for his illustrations to accompany the text. It is now offered to those who appreciate all of heaven's treasures. Biblical quotations are from the Authorized Version, unless otherwise noted.

Francis of Assisi

Introduction

"**I**s my dog in heaven?"

That was my question as a teenager when Brownie died. It sent me on the quest.

Brownie and I began life together as "puppies" and grew up companions. He walked me to school and faithfully waited for me in the afternoons until school let out. At about five years of age, I decided to run away from home for an adventure; Brownie ran with me, and he also rode home with me in the patrol car. We rarely separated.

Brownie was a playmate, friend, drier of childhood tears with a moist tongue, and personal guardian. I recall snuggling between his paws, pouring out sobs of self-pity to what I knew was his sympathetic ear. Brownie was my buddy. When he died, there seemed no question that we would have the same hope and the same reward at the end of our lives.

When Brownie died, my assumption was challenged. I heard: "Animals do not have souls," "They are just dumb beasts," "Heaven is for people," and variations on those themes. I could not accept such pronouncements uncritically. To me, they didn't ring true for Brownie.

Animals had been a significant part of my growing up. My grandmother and a nearby cousin raised chickens, ducks, guineas, goats, cows, mules, and horses. I spent most of my childhood with these animal friends. Such an array of friends could not be lost forever.

I felt such a strong bonding with animals, and my memories of them remain fond and dear—memories of feelings shared and of personalities observed. Oscar the pig always ambling to his fence and calling me to come and chat with him. Maude the mule keeping a vigilant eye on me. Each time I appeared, she sauntered over to visit.

The chickens and I played games together. A favorite of mine was my version of "Rock-a-bye Baby." Holding a chicken in the palms of both hands and gently rocking back and forth until the hen closed her eyes in sleep, I could place her head under her wing and cradle her like a baby. I discovered in this game that as you rock a chicken's body, the head remains stationary. Those chickens were so trusting of me that I could visit even the nesting hens and they would be unperturbed.

I still remember those animals of my childhood by name and personality. They were special, and they were friends. They bent a sympathetic ear and listened patiently and eagerly to my fantasies and troubles. I think of Bossie, my grandmother's old heifer; when listening to one of my sad childhood tales of woe, I saw a tear roll from her big, sympathetic eye. Brownie wasn't the only one whose eternity I questioned. These animal friends simply could not be lost forever.

Apparently, I am not alone in this feeling. Over the years, when friends have lost pets who were like family to them, they invariably ask if those pets are in heaven. To these of us, it seems if we go to heaven, they go to heaven. In fact, if it is heaven, they must be there.

When I first saw a figure of Francis of Assisi holding a bird resting in his hand and glancing kindly toward it, I felt an affinity at once. Later, I discovered depictions of him with many different animals, such as dogs, lambs, and deer ... I felt a bond with this man from the thirteenth century.

When I read *The Little Flowers of Saint Francis*, a record of his life by members of his order, I confirmed the sense of kinship. His celebration of all God's creation and his belief that God created every animal to reflect an element of the Creator and to teach us about Himself found a witness of truth in my spirit.

In the experiences of Francis, I felt support for my instinctive feeling about Brownie. I learned why Francis is always depicted with a bird. In *The Little Flowers*, there is a report of Francis on one of his journeys through the countryside. Upon viewing a field of thousands of birds of a variety of species, he felt compelled to preach to them.

The saint called on the birds to be grateful to God that they may fly so freely wherever they will, are clothed in coats of such beauty, have beautiful voices with which to sing, and are provided without sowing or toiling for their food. The report is that the birds gathered around him, listened intently as he spoke, and burst into beautiful song when he finished.

There are other reports of Francis and the birds. Once he rescued some doves from a boy taking them to be sold at market. He sent them on their way with instruction to be grateful to God for their rescue. On another occasion, he commanded the noisy swallows of Alviano to be quiet that he might speak to the crowd gathered in the square. They fell silent and listened intently to him as he preached.

The significant feature in these reports is that to Francis and to those who observed and reported these instances, the creatures seemed aware of and responsive to a message about their Creator. To these observers, it was not meaningless to preach to animals.

A report from the same time period explains how Anthony of Padua preached to the fish of Rimini. The report says that the fish gathered by thousands from the sea and the river's mouth at Rimini to listen carefully to Anthony's sermon, responding with joy. Again, the minimal significance of these instances is that to the participants and those who recorded these events, there was considered appropriateness to preaching to the creatures. Here is evidence at least as far back as the thirteenth century of a tradition of the gospel for the creatures. Is there a firm foundation for such a tradition?

With my obvious sympathies, through the years I came to be known among friends as "an animal lover." Acquaintances as well as strangers who have lost pets have asked me the question, "Is my pet in heaven?" I am not alone in wanting the question answered. But the answer must be more than a strong personal opinion, even if shared by so saintly a figure as Francis of Assisi. To be of real value and comfort, the answer must have a sound footing with a firm assurance.

I believe that such an answer must be in biblical revelation. The Bible is where we find the certainty for the hope of heaven and eternity. I look in the Bible for the definitive word and our dependable answer. I sense an answer is definitely needed. When reading the concluding chapter in Cleveland Amory's *The Best Cat Ever*, he records his loss of Polar Bear and his struggle with grief and his encounters with others similarly struggling. He relates an argument with a priest who told him animals didn't have souls and couldn't go to heaven. I had just published the first edition to this book and immediately sent a copy to Mr. Amory.

By return mail, I received the following letter:

Dear Mr. Hunt,

Thanks so very much not only for sending me *Is My Dog in Heaven?* but for writing it in the first place. If ever a book cried out to be written, it is this. Quite apart from taking comfort from your book, I thoroughly enjoyed reading about the various dogs of your life, most especially the current Huskies. These have always been favorites of mine so you can readily understand how I fell completely under the spell of Barnabas and Mary Agnes.

Because you are such a good friend of animals, I am taking the liberty of enclosing our latest bulletin. I think you might enjoy reading about some of the things we have been doing for our four-legged friends.

In closing, my thanks again for sharing your *Is My Dog in Heaven?* with me.

With warmest regards,
Cleveland Amory

The Lion and the Lamb

CHAPTER 1

Creatures, Creation, and Recreation

The Bible opens with the creation story and the Creator God calling forth out of nothing light and darkness, the heavens, the earth, and the sea. Next, this setting of the world is populated with "every living creature which moveth within the waters," "every winged of the air," and "every creeping thing and beast of the earth." Finally, God completes His creation with man (Genesis 1).

God calls this creation "very good." When completed, God rests and takes His pleasure. This is obviously creation as God desires it to be. A striking feature of this creation in Eden is the harmony that prevails between man and all nature, particularly between man and the creatures. Man is given the role of custodian of the creatures and is told to name each in turn.

The task as namer for the creatures holds a deep significance. In Hebrew consciousness, a name is the embodiment of the nature of the named. The giving of a name implies a special relationship to the subject. For instance, when Abram entered a covenant relationship with God, he was renamed Abraham (Genesis 17:5). When Jacob wrestled with an angel through the night and prevailed, he was renamed Israel (Genesis 32:28). This tradition continues into the New Testament period when Simon became Peter and when Saul was renamed Paul (Matthew 16:17–18; Acts 9:4).

Names among Hebrews are never casually or arbitrarily given. They signify something about the nature or task of the named and the relationship with the namer. "Thou shalt call his name Jesus for he shall save his people from their sins" (Matthew 1:21).

It is this Eden of man and creatures in which man's rebellion interrupts and corrupts, making redemption a necessity. If sin had not intervened, Eden would appear today as God originally ordained it: humans in harmony with the creatures and with all the world around them. This is the paradise lost; paradise regained will return to God's original intention.

This is explicit as the biblical revelation draws to its close and John sees God's restoration of His creation as "a new heaven and a new earth" (Revelation 21:1). This presence of all creatures in God's ideal once more appears in "the coming down from God of the holy city, the new Jerusalem" (Revelation 21:2).

Their presence is seen as John receives a glimpse into heaven. In his first vision of God's throne, John sees "every creature which is in heaven and on the earth and under the earth and such as are in the sea, and all that are in them." John hears the creatures saying, "Blessing and honor and glory and power be unto him that sitteth upon the throne and unto the Lamb for ever and ever" (Revelation 5:13).

The word translated as "creature" is the same one used to denote all the living things that God made. John's vision is of all creatures in God's presence and joined in the worship and praise of heaven.

In the final vision of God's redemption fulfilled, John writes, "And he that sat upon the throne said, 'Behold, I make all things new'" (Revelation 21:5). This "all things" (*pas*) used here means "all things that exist, all things created," and it is the same word that is translated in the prologue to John's Gospel when speaking of the Word who was in the beginning—"*all things* were made by him and without him was not anything made that was made" (John 1:3; emphasis added). It is also the word used when Paul writes that in Christ "*all things* are become new" (2 Corinthians 5:17; emphasis added).

The presence of all creatures in John's vision of heaven, including their participation in heaven's worship and in the celebration of the glory of God, is the culmination of a theme consistent throughout the biblical revelation.

In the eighth century before Christ, the prophet Isaiah pictured the coming day of the Lord's fulfillment of His redemptive work:

> The wolf also shall dwell with the Lamb, and the leopard shall lie down with the kid; and the calf and the young lion and the fatling together; and a little child shall lead them. And the cow and the bear shall feed; their young ones shall lie down together: and the lion shall eat straw like the ox. And the suckling child shall play on the hole of the asp, and the weaned child shall put his hand on the cockatrice's den. They shall not hurt nor destroy in all my holy mountain: for the earth shall be full of the knowledge of the Lord, as the waters cover the sea. (Isaiah 11:6–9)

Quite clearly, Isaiah's picture of the day of the Lord describes all creation in harmony, as it first originated in Eden. The picture definitely includes every creature.

A century later, the prophet heralding the end of the Babylonian captivity likewise pictures the coming day of the Lord's redemption:

> The wolf and the lamb shall feed together, and the lion shall eat straw like the bullock; and dust shall be the serpent's meat. They shall not hurt nor destroy in all my holy mountain, saith the Lord. (Isaiah 65:25)

A striking feature explicit in this passage and in the one previously noted is the new state of harmony among the creatures themselves. Specific phrases combine to declare a reign of peace among the creatures and an end to their predatory existence. "The wolf shall dwell with the lamb." "The leopard shall lie down with the kid." "The cow and the bear shall feed." "Their young ones shall lie together." "The lion shall eat straw like he ox." "They shall not hurt nor destroy." Peace at last.

The contrast between the present state of nature and that of the peaceable kingdom in Isaiah is a commentary on the extent of the corruption of creation as a result of the fall of man. It produced chaos in the natural order and enmity among the creatures. Isaiah's peaceable kingdom is for me the ideal picture of heaven's tranquility—all creation in harmony.

The hymnbook of Israel continues the tradition of the inclusion of all creatures and creation in the celebration of God. "The earth is the Lord's and the fullness thereof, the world and they that dwell therein" (Psalm 24:1). Thus, when singing God's praise, all creation is called to join in the chorus:

> Sing to the Lord, *all* the earth!
> All the earth shall worship thee and sing unto thee.
> (Psalm 66:1, 4; emphasis added)

> Let the heaven and earth praise him, the seas, and *everything that moveth therein*. (Psalm 69:34; emphasis added)

> Let the heavens rejoice, and let the earth be glad: let the sea roar *and the fullness thereof*. Let the field be joyful, and *all that is therein*: then shall all the trees of the wood rejoice before the Lord. (Psalm 96:11–13; emphasis added)

> The Lord reigneth; let the earth rejoice.
> The heavens declare his righteousness. (Psalm 97:1, 6)

> Make a joyful noise unto the Lord, *all* the earth: make a loud noise, and rejoice, and sing praise.
> Let the sea roar, *and the fullness thereof*; the world, and *they that dwell therein*. Let the floods clap their hands: let the hills be joyful together before the Lord. (Psalm 98:4, 7–9; emphasis added)

> Praise ye the Lord. Praise ye the Lord from the heavens: praise him in the heights.

> Praise ye him, all his angels: praise ye him, all ye stars of light.

Praise him, ye heavens of heavens, and ye waters that be above the heavens.
Let them praise the name of the Lord: for he commanded and they were created.

He hath also stablished them for ever and ever:
he hath made a decree which shall not pass.
Praise the Lord from the earth, ye dragons, and all deeps:
Fire, and hail; snow, and vapour; stormy wind fulfilling his word:
Mountains, and all hills; fruitful trees, and all cedars:
Beasts, and all cattle; creeping things, and flying fowl:
Kings of the earth, and all people; princes and all judges of the earth:
Both young men, and maidens; old men, and children:
Let them praise the name of the Lord: for his name alone is excellent; his glory is above the earth and heaven.
He also exalteth the horn of his people, the praise of all his saints; even of the children of Israel, a people near unto him. Praise ye the Lord. (Psalm 148; emphasis added)

And this is the verse with which the book of Psalms ends: "Let *everything that hath breath* praise the Lord. Praise ye the Lord" (Psalm 150:6; emphasis added).

In Israel's book of worship, there is a clear sense of all creatures and all creation caught up in the celebration and praise of God, especially the celebration of God the Redeemer. The phrases "all the earth" and "all that dwell therein" are all-inclusive. The praise of all the creatures is loudly heard in the coming day of the Lord.

The songs of Isaiah celebrate the redemptive work of God's suffering servant and the coming Messiah. These include, "The mountains and the hills shall break forth before you into singing, and all the trees of the field shall clap their hands. Instead of the thorn shall come up the fig tree, and instead of the brier shall come up the myrtle tree: and it shall be to the Lord for a name, for an *everlasting* sign that shall not be cut off" (Isaiah 55:12–13; emphasis added). Eden is restored!

This peaceable kingdom of God's restored creation has a foretaste in *The Little Flowers of Saint Francis.* In the village of Gubbio, villagers feel frightened of a wolf who terrorizes their town. Francis visits the village. He encounters the wolf, who surprisingly comes to him with humbleness and submissiveness. Francis brings the townspeople and the wolf together, negotiating a pact between them. The wolf no longer ravishes the village or their herds, but he visits their homes each morning to be fed as a household pet. The villagers celebrate this peace with the wolf as a goodness of the Lord.

In the Sermon on the Mount, Jesus uses an illustration that assumes an agreement among his hearers about God's providential care of the creatures: "Behold the fowls of the air; they sow not, neither do they reap, nor gather into barns; yet your heavenly Father feedeth them" (Matthew 6:26). And later, more pointedly, he says, "Are not two sparrows sold for a farthing? And one of them shall not fall on the ground without your Father" (Matthew 10:29). Jesus assumes that the heavenly Father provides for the creatures.

Long ago, the psalmist had declared plainly "the Lord preserveth both man and beast" (Psalm 36:6). In the biblical revelation, God's creatures are envisioned in God's world at creation as well as in that world's recreation. They are participants in God's worship, praise, and the celebration of His redemptive glory.

Eden, Isaiah's Day of the Lord, Israel's songs of praise and celebration, John's vision of heaven—the creatures are included in all of these. God's redemption is a restoration of Eden, the renewal of His original "good" creation. This is how God made it and how God will reinstate His ultimate fulfillment of creation. The creatures are in Eden at creation; they are restored to Eden at the recreation.

Creatures and the Covenant

CHAPTER 2
Creatures and the Covenant

I n the Old Testament, there are two mighty acts of God
that serve as prototypes for God's work of redemption: the
Great Flood of Noah's time and the Exodus of the Children
of Israel from Egypt.

In addition, we have the covenant into which God enters
with Israel at Sinai as the basis for God's being their god and
they being His people. This covenant serves as prologue to the
new covenant in Jesus Christ. These are the Bible's revelations
of God's redemption and promise of heaven. The creatures
clearly are included in all these promises for the future.

The Great Flood

One does not recall God's covenant with Noah without
picturing the parade of animals entering the ark. God gives
Noah instructions for the building of the ark as means of
rescue from God's impending judgment on sinful man. God
commands Noah to take his family aboard the ark to be saved
from the flood.

"And of every living thing of all flesh, two of every sort shalt thou bring into the ark, to keep them alive with thee; they shall be male and female. Of fowls after their kind, and of cattle after their kind, of every creeping thing of the earth after his kind, two of every sort shall come unto thee, to keep them alive." (Genesis 6:19–20)

As the ark floats upon the flood, it is noted, "And God remembered Noah and every living thing and all the cattle that was with him in the ark" (Genesis 8:1). When the ark lands, "Every beast, every creeping thing, and every fowl, and whatsoever creepeth upon the earth, after their kinds, went forth out of the ark" (Genesis 8:19).

The flood is God's judgment. The ark stands as God's provision of rescue from that judgment (redemption). The passengers aboard the ark are the redeemed. As Noah's family represents mankind, so every living thing is likewise represented aboard the ark.

The intention is more explicit than the symbolism of the ark and its passengers. After the disembarkation from the ark, God declares:

"And I, behold, I establish my covenant with you, and with your seed after you; And with every living creature that is with you, of the fowl, of the cattle, and of every beast of the earth with you; from all that go out of the ark, to every beast of the earth. And I will establish my covenant with you, neither shall all flesh be cut off any more by the waters of a flood; neither shall there any more be a flood to destroy the earth." (Genesis 9:9–11)

As God sets the rainbow in the sky as the symbol of this covenant, He reiterates with whom this covenant is established:

> "And God said, This is the token of the covenant which I make between me and you and every living creature that is with you, *for a perpetual generation.*" (Genesis 9:12; emphasis added)

It is unmistakable that "every living creature" is included in the redemption of Noah's flood. There is also explicit assurance that the promise made in the covenant after the flood stands perpetually.

The Exodus

In the deliverance from Egyptian bondage into the land of promise, we find the symbolic inclusion of God's creatures. Pharaoh inquires for whom Moses requests permission to depart. "And Moses said, We will go with our young and with our old, with our sons and with our daughters, with our flocks and with our herds will we go" (Exodus 10:9). Moses later adds, "Our cattle also shall go with us; there shall not a hoof be left behind" (Exodus 10:26).

In each plague by which Moses sought Pharaoh's permission for departure, it is specifically noted that if a plague might threaten Israel's cattle and flocks, they are to be spared from its consequences (Exodus 9:4, 19; 11:7).

More significant is the final plague of the angel of death passing over the land, sparing the firstborn of all those who have the blood of the lamb sprinkled upon the doorways of their houses. The cattle and flocks of Israel are also spared by the blood of the lamb in this night of Passover.

Afterward, the Lord declared, "Sanctify unto me all the first-born, whatsoever openeth the womb among the children of Israel, both of man and of beast: it is mine" (Exodus 13:2). In the Exodus from Egypt, the animals of Israel are included in the request to be set free, they are spared judgment by the blood of the Lamb, and they cross the Red Sea from the land of bondage to the land of promise. They are partakers of every element of the redemptive symbolism. Afterward, God specifically includes them with those who are to be "sanctified" or set aside for Him.

The Sinai Covenant

The Law given to Moses on Mount Sinai is addressed to the obedience of man. After all, the need for redemption has been predicated by the disobedience of man. These commandments reveal how God wishes it to be in His world. The relationship God desires between Himself and man and between men is quite clearly defined.

At a significant point in the commandments, animals are included. It is in the fourth commandment requiring that the Sabbath day be kept holy. There is an enumeration of those whom this commandment enjoins. Those specified are "thou, thy son, thy daughter, thy manservant, thy maidservant, *thy cattle*, and thy stranger within thy gates" (Exodus 20:10).

The injunction calls for the cattle to keep that day holy, as day is described as "the Sabbath of the Lord thy God" (Exodus 20:10), a day which the Lord blessed and hallowed (Exodus 20:11). In other words, animals are to share in the Lord's Sabbath.

The significance of this invitation is seen when one considers the meaning of the Sabbath. This is the only commandment for which a rationale is given:

"For in six days the Lord made heaven and earth, the sea, and all that in them is, and rested the seventh day." (Exodus 20:11)

Thus Sabbath rest becomes participation in and commemoration of that rest of the Lord after completion of the work of creation. This rest does not convey a sense of recovery from the weariness of creative labors. God is and has ever been the God who "neither sleeps nor slumbers" (Psalm 121:4). Rather His rest is satisfaction—shalom, peace—at the completion of something very good. That the seventh day is the Sabbath of the Lord forms a basis for the number seven coming to represent in Hebrew consciousness the idea of fullness and completion.

The seventh day, the Sabbath, is the day God celebrates His pleasure at the completion of His "good creation." Satisfaction and joy in the creation is behind God's blessing and sanctifying this day (Genesis 2:3). In the Sinai covenant, God invites the creation to celebrate the Sabbath as a prototype and foreshadowing of the restoration of God's creation. It is a participation in the expectation of redemption. This is the commandment in which God specifies the cattle to be included.

As a symbol in time, God calls for one day in each seven to mark the promise and expectation of redemption. Likewise, one year in each seven years is specified as a Sabbath year and is to include "thy cattle" and "the beasts that are in thy land" (Leviticus 25:7). That portion of the Sinai covenant, the Sabbath observance, which is commemoration of God's completion and fulfilling of His creation, calls for inclusion of the creatures.

Through Hosea, the prophet of the eighth century before Christ, God reiterates His inclusion of the creatures in His covenant:

> "And in that day will I make a covenant for them with the beasts of the field and with the fowls of heaven, and with the creeping things of the ground: and I will break the bow and the sword and the battle out of the earth, and will make them to lie down safely." (Hosea 2:18)

It is very clear that the creatures are represented in the redemption of the ark in the Great Flood and in the Exodus from Egyptian bondage—those mighty acts of God foreshadowing the redemption of the world. They are beneficiaries of the covenants made with Noah and made with Moses and the children of Israel at Sinai. This is the background of God's new covenant in Jesus Christ.

The New Covenant in Christ

The more familiar proclamations of the good news in Jesus Christ are:

> "For God so loved the world, that he gave his only begotten Son, that whosoever believeth in him should not perish, but have everlasting life. For God sent not his Son into the world to condemn the world; but that the world through him might be saved." (John 3:16–17)

"God was in Christ reconciling the world unto himself." (2 Corinthians 3:19)

And there is that proclamation with which the ministry of Jesus begins:

> "The next day John seeth Jesus coming unto him, and saith, Behold the Lamb of God, which taketh away the sin of the world." (John 1:29)

There is one reoccurring word designating the object of God's redemptive work in Christ. "God so loved the *world*," "not to condemn the *world*," "that the *world* through him might be saved," "reconciling the *world* unto himself," "taketh away the sin of the *world*." Christ's work of redemption is for "the world."

Wherever the word translated as "world" is used in the New Testament, it is understood to be inclusive of all God's creation. It is intended for the world, which definitely includes the creatures.

When describing the effect of Christ's coming, the apostle Paul writes:

> "Therefore if any man be in Christ, he is a new creature: old things are passed away; behold, *all things are become new.*" (2 Corinthians 5:17)

A more explicit passage in which Paul is particularly addressing the subject of the redemption of creation and the creatures is:

> "For the earnest expectation of the creature waiteth for the manifestation of the sons of God. For the

creature was made subject to vanity, not willingly, but by reason of him who hath subjected the same in hope, because *the creature itself also shall be delivered from the bondage of corruption into the glorious liberty of the children of God.* For we know that *the whole creation groaneth and travaileth in pain together until now.* And not only they, but ourselves also, which have the firstfruits of the Spirit, even we ourselves groan within ourselves, *waiting for the adoption, to wit, the redemption of our body.*" (Romans 8:19–23)

This is a traditional translation of this passage, but a modern paraphrase of it remains true to its implication but is more explicit:

For all creation is waiting patiently and hopefully for that future day[a] when God will resurrect his children. For on that day thorns and thistles, sin, death, and decay—the things that overcame the world against its will at God's command—will all disappear, and the world around us will share in the glorious freedom from sin which God's children enjoy.

For we know that even the things of nature, like animals and plants, suffer in sickness and death as they await this great event and even we Christians, although we have the Holy Spirit within us as a foretaste of future glory, also groan to be released from pain and suffering. We, too, wait anxiously for that day when God will give us our full rights as his children, including the new bodies he has promised us—bodies that will never be sick again and will never die. (The Living Bible)

Paul also writes to the Church at Colossae, speaking of God the Father:

> "Who hath delivered us from the power of darkness, and hath translated us into the kingdom of his dear Son: in whom we have redemption through his blood, even the forgiveness of sins: who is the image of the invisible God, *the firstborn of every creature*: for by him were all things created, that are in heaven, and that are in earth, visible and invisible, whether they be thrones, or dominions, or principalities, or powers: *all things* were created *by* him, and *for* him ... by him *all things* consist ... that in *all things* he might have the preeminence. For it pleased the Father that in him should *all fulness* dwell. And, having made peace through the blood of his cross, by him *to reconcile all things unto himself*, by him, I say, whether they be things in earth, or things in heaven." (Colossians 1:13–20; emphasis added)

How emphatic could the New Testament be that the creatures are in Christ's redemption? They share in the rescue from the flood of Noah's time and in the release from Egyptian bondage in Moses's day, the two mighty acts of God's redemption. They are included in the perpetual promise of God's covenant with Noah and in the Sabbath rest of the Sinai covenant. And they are among all things Christ has reconciled to himself.

Animals as Sacrifice and Image

CHAPTER 3

Animals as Sacrifice and Image

When one thinks of animals in the scriptures, there comes to mind most readily their inclusion aboard Noah's ark and then their place in Israel's sacrificial system. The two pictures seem at odds.

Israel was instructed to bring to the priest offerings of their cattle, herds, and flocks (Leviticus 1:2). The focal point in the court of the tabernacle, and later the temple, to which the congregation of Israel came for their feasts and celebration of God was the altar upon which these sacrifices were made.

A peace offering was to be from the herd (Leviticus 3:1); a sin offering, a young bullock (Leviticus 4:3); a trespass offering, a lamb or kid of the goats (Leviticus 5:6). The Book of Leviticus details the offerings acceptable, their preparation for and method of sacrifice as well as the disposition of the sacrificial remains.

The most prominent sacrifice in Israel's worship was the Passover Lamb, which had enabled the Exodus from Egypt. The blood of that lamb rescued God's people from death and permitted their deliverance from captivity to the land of promise. That lamb would ever afterward be remembered and commemorated in the high festival of the Jewish year. This symbol of the Passover Lamb remains central in Jewish worship to this day.

As the Hebrew experience of God continued and their understanding of God became fuller, awareness grew in Israel's consciousness that animal sacrifice was not the will of God and what He required of His people. As early as the reign of Israel's first king, the prophet Samuel declared:

> "And Samuel said, Hath the Lord as great delight in burnt offerings and sacrifices as in obeying the voice of the Lord? Behold, to obey is better than sacrifice and to hearken than the fat of rams." (1 Samuel 15:22)

This consciousness continued to grow with God's people:

> "Sacrifice and offering thou didst not desire; mine ears hast thou opened: burnt offering and sin offering hast thou not required." (Psalm 40:6)

> "For thou desirest not sacrifice; else would I give it: thou delightest not in burnt offerings. The sacrifices of God are a broken spirit: a broken and a contrite heart, O God, thou wilt not despise." (Psalm 51:16–17)

There comes an increasing awareness that what God requires of man is not something to be brought and left with Him, but rather God's desire is that man offer something of himself.

> "To do justice and judgment is more acceptable to the Lord than sacrifice." (Proverbs 21:3)

This awareness becomes a conviction of the will of God in the prophets of the eighth and seventh century before Christ.

> "I have desired mercy and not sacrifice; and the knowledge of God more than burnt offerings." (Hosea 6:6)

> "I hate, I despise your feast days, and I will not smell your solemn assemblies. Though you offer me burnt offerings and your meat offerings, I will not accept them: neither will I regard the peace offerings of your fat beasts. Take thou away from me the noise of thy songs; for I will not hear the melody of thy viols. But let judgment run down as waters and righteousness as a mighty stream." (Amos 5:21–24)

The conviction takes root as Jeremiah hears God declare: "your burnt offerings are not acceptable nor your sacrifices sweet unto me" (Jeremiah 6:20). The prophet Micah concludes:

> "Wherewith shall I come before the Lord and bow myself before the high God? Shall I come before him with burnt offerings, with calves of a year old? Will the Lord be pleased with thousands of rams or with ten thousands of rivers of oil? Shall I give my first-born for my transgression, the fruit of my body for the sin of my soul? He hath showed thee, O man, what is good; and what doeth the Lord require of thee but to do justly, and to love mercy, and to walk humbly with thy God?" (Micah 6:6–8)

As regards animal sacrifice, the faith of Israel progressively draws closer to that position found in the new covenant in Jesus Christ:

> "I beseech you, therefore, brethren, that you present your bodies a living sacrifice" (Romans 12:1).

> "let us offer the sacrifice of praise to God continually, that is, the fruit of our lips giving thanks to his name. But to do good and to communicate forget not: for with such sacrifices God is well pleased." (Hebrews 13:15–16)

With the fuller understanding of God's will, it becomes increasingly clear that the offering of animal sacrifices is not pleasing or acceptable to God.

This might seem to the modern mind a higher appreciation of the value of animals. However, that is not necessarily so. We have a different sensitivity to cruelty and a sense of response to God fashioned by the moral climate created by the teachings of Jesus.

Were we able to share the same frame of reference and values of the ancient mind without the fullness of light revealed in Jesus Christ, we might better appreciate the meaning of animal sacrifice in that time and, therefore, the regard of the animals offered.

Our modern definition of sacrifice has undergone subtle adjustment across time. It now involves connotations of "giving something up, destroying, or foregoing." The emphasis is on denying and surrender. The implications of the word are essentially negative.

We are now too schooled in the theology of grace and unmerited salvation to fathom appreciably the frame of mind if one were without it. If that were our condition and then we knew that there should be something we might offer by which such unattainable benefit might be ours, would we not offer it with eagerness and joy? This was the religious condition of the ancient Hebrew. His sacrifice gave him the same thrill that is ours in the acceptance of the reconciliation to God through Jesus Christ.

The ancient sacrifice was not a cast-off, disposable value. On the contrary, the sacrificial instructions include every insistence to assure its value. The repeated description of the offering is that it must be "without blemish" (Exodus 12:5; Leviticus 5:15). It must be the best.

Far more significant is the understanding of the value the sacrificed animals represented to the Lord. The striking feature of the sacrificial system is that the animals were "a sacrifice for man's sin," and able to make "atonement for sin." By them, sin was forgiven (Leviticus 5:14–18). On Israel's Day of Atonement, a scapegoat upon whom the priest laid hands bore all the people's iniquities and "all their transgressions in all their sins" (Leviticus 16:21).

The only other in biblical revelation who God would accept as an atonement for man's sin and by whom He would forgive sin is His Son Jesus Christ (John 3:16–17). In the created order, none other than animals were given such an exalted position of representation. The animal sacrifices are described as "pleasing to the Lord" (Leviticus 8:21) and declared to be "most holy" (Leviticus 6:17; 7:1, 6). Animals have an exalted position in the sacrificial system. They are prototypes of the Christ and are, in fact, the symbols and instruments of God's redemption.

The pleasing and acceptable regard in which the ancients believed God held animals continues in the consciousness of

Israel beyond the sacrificial system into the New Testament. The psalmist believed God preserved the beasts. They were continually included in the celebration songs of God's glory and goodness until the time when Jesus assured that no sparrow falls without God's awareness.

The more telling evidence of this divine regard is the appropriateness with which animals are seen as images of God. We already noted that animals in the sacrificial system were prototypes of Christ's work of atonement. One of the dominant symbols by which Christ is identified is as the Lamb of God, the Christian Passover Lamb, releasing mankind from captivity to freedom by the offering up of Himself.

John the Baptist introduces Jesus at the beginning of His ministry: "Behold the Lamb of God who takes away the sin of the world" (John 1:29). Note once more "the world" as the object of the redemptive work.

Jesus is also referred to as "the Lion of Judah" (Revelation 5:5). In other subtle ways, an affinity for animals must be inferred from Jesus's identification of Himself as the Good Shepherd (John 10:14), a role inescapably associated with the care of sheep.

There is no avoiding the animal connection with the incarnation of the Redeemer God. The first public proclamation of the coming of the Messiah is to shepherds "keeping watch over their flocks" (Luke 2:8), and Christ is born in a stable and cradled in a manger (Luke 2:7). The Bread of Life first rests in the feeding place of animals.

The third person of the Trinity, the Holy Spirit, is symbolized as a descending dove (Mark 1:10 and parallel passages). The dove is the only concrete symbol in the New Testament of the Holy Spirit.

Even God the Father, the Jehovah of the Old Testament,

for whom it is strictly forbidden that there should be any image or "likeness of anything that is in heaven above or that is in the earth beneath or that is in the water under the earth" (Exodus 20:4), is described by similes to animals. He is described "like as a lion and a young lion roaring" (Isaiah 31:4–5) and as a leopard and "a bear that is bereaved of her whelps" (Hosea 13:7–8).

God's special regard for animals is unmistakable when they are described as "pleasing to the Lord" and "holy to the Lord." They must have extraordinary value to God that He should find them acceptable to merit His forgiveness of man. It would be God's only Son who would greater fulfill that role. Also there must be an affinity for them in their appropriateness as images to convey to us something of the divine nature and work.

Their place in the sacrificial system was quite the opposite of disregard for their value. Only the work of Christ and the repentance and obedience of man could be of greater redemptive value. From the beginning, animals have been continuously involved both as objects for and symbols of God's redemptive work.

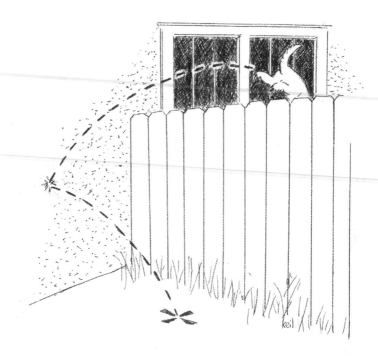

Barnabas and the Fence

CHAPTER 4

Do Animals Have Souls?

"**A**nimals don't have souls!"

I've heard this statement declared with finality, and I've wondered how it became so unquestionable a truth for the speaker. There is no biblical text to affirm it. Yet there are some who believe it and consider it proof that animals can't possibly partake of eternal life.

The dictum seems more proof of the degree of secularization of some theology. The immortality of the soul as a prerequisite to eternity is not a Christian concept, nor a Jewish one, but more a product of Greek philosophy or Eastern mysticism. It originates in Plato's teachings rather than in scripture. The Christian basis of eternity rests on the resurrection of the body, not on the indestructibility of an aspect of our being that we call "the soul." The Christian creed from the beginning has been an affirmation of belief "in the resurrection of the body" (The Apostles' Creed, the Nicene Creed, etc.).

The distinction between man with soul and animals without may have been fostered by biblical translators' choice of words. The King James authorized version of the Scriptures of 1611 translates the Hebrew word *nephest* in Genesis 2:7 as "living soul":

> And the Lord God formed man of the dust of the ground, and breathed into his nostrils the breathe of life; and man became *a living soul.*

Yet when referring to creatures, the same word is translated differently:

> And God said, Let the earth bring forth *the living creature* after his kind, cattle, and creeping thing and beast of the earth after his kind: and it was so. (Genesis 1:24)

It would have been as linguistically valid to translate the former "and man became *a living creature*" and the latter, "Let the earth bring forth *the living soul* after his kind." The difference is in the choice of the translator according to his reading of the context. In the Hebrew text, the words are identical.

This word *nephest* means in Hebrew "soul, life, person, living being, blood, breath, living creature" and is translated in English versions according to the choice of the translator. It is used of man as in Genesis 2:7 and Genesis 2:19. It is likewise used in reference to animals as in Genesis 1:20, 24, 30 and Genesis 9:12, 15, 16. The English translations sometimes make a distinction that is not necessarily made in the original text.

Translators' choices together with Greek influence (the immortality of the soul) on Western thought may have drastically contributed to the distinction. A sharp distinction is not clearly defined in the biblical texts.

However, there is an aspect of being that is other than the physical designated in scripture by "soul." This is apparent in texts such as:

> And now, Israel, what does the Lord thy God require of thee but to fear the Lord thy God, to walk in all his ways and to love him and to serve him with all thy heart and with all thy soul. (Deuteronomy 10:12)

The same distinction is likewise found in the New Testament:

> And thou shalt love the Lord thy God with all thy heart and with all thy soul and with all thy mind and with all thy strength: this is the first commandment. (Mark 12:30)

Through the centuries, it has been the burden of theology to define what is the soul. There has been uniform agreement that this soul is the nonphysical quality of existence, and the greater majority of theologians have concluded that the soul of man is not a separate entity from the spirit of man; in other words, man is not trichotomic.

> That man consist of soul and body, ought not to be controverted. By "soul" I understand an immortal, yet created essence, which is the nobler part of him. Sometimes it is called a "spirit"; for though when these names are connected, they have a different signification, yet when "spirit" is used separately, it means the same as "soul." (John Calvin, *Institutes*, book 1, chapter XV)

The consensus of biblical scholarship and theology has found the soul discernible through its faculties or attributes, and most have found these best defined in the capacity for knowing and willing.

> The human soul has two faculties which relate to our present design, the understanding and the will. Now, let it be the office of the understanding to discriminate between objects, as they shall respectively appear deserving of approbation or disapprobation; but of the will, to choose and follow what the understanding shall have pronounced to be good; to abhor and avoid what it shall have condemned. (John Calvin, Ibid.)

As Calvin also points out in the work cited, these faculties of the soul are inclusive of understanding, reason, imagination, will, and the irascible and concupiscible faculties (i.e., strong emotions). In other words, the presence of the soul is confirmed by the presence of reason, emotion, and decision.

I have experienced all these faculties in animals I have known. And I have encountered multi-evidence of them in animals about whom I have read and heard.

My Siberian husky, Barnabas, repeatedly demonstrates his ability to reason. He resents being confined in a fenced yard. He has nowhere to go, nor does he wish to run away; whenever he "escapes" the fenced area, he immediately comes to the house entrance to scratch on the door for re-admittance to the house. It is clear he is making a point: he is not going to be fenced in.

We live in a city with leash laws and busy thoroughfares. To me, our fencing is essential; to Barnabas, it is an effrontery and an infringement. Barnabas and I continuously face off in a battle of the wits. From the first, he sought and found ways to circumvent the fence. He has found every weakness and frailty in its structure. He is an expert climber, and we have gone from a six-foot to an eight-foot fence. After months of this war of the fence, it seemed I had won. For nearly a week, I relished my victory when I heard a scratch on the front door. I opened it, and Barnabas paraded triumphantly into the house. I vainly searched the fence for its weakness. Meanwhile, Barnabas emphasized his master with that scratch on the front door.

Nearly certain he had outwitted me, one day I stood looking out my window. I noticed Barnabas in the corner of the yard behaving very curiously. I watched unseen. After a careful survey of the situation, he took off from the corner in a hurried dash toward the house. A few feet away, he leaped into the air, landed against the house, pushed off from it, did a sideways flip in midair, and sailed over the fence where it joined the house. I was amazed. Such an acrobatic feat could not have been accomplished without careful reasoning and planning. There had been no model to imitate.

I regularly take my dogs to our place in the country, a 125-mile journey that usually lasts hours. Barnabas knows the route well. He also associates the clicking of the turn indicator with our turns. When we approach a usual turn, he will look at the indicator until I put it on. Whenever I turn it on at an expected place, he immediately looks left and right to see where we could be turning.

Another of my huskies, Mary Agnes, has also learned that route. Her particular affinity is for cows. She knows on our journey the pastures where they usually are. Before they come into view, she is ready at the window. If I should see a herd at some unaccustomed place and she is not on alert, I merely say, "Cows." She jumps to her post.

On our journeys, all my dogs know when we are within the last few miles of our destination. The excitement and anticipation builds as we approach. They also know if I detour or make unusual side trips. Their curiosity and inquiry are evident. They look at me, and they look in the direction of our travel with clear expressions of puzzlement.

Sarah, the mother of my husky litter, has always been especially fond of our place in the country and had a special affection for a cousin, Benji, who lived there. She unmistakably preferred him to me. When we were there on visits and she perceived that the time for departing was near, she would slip off and hide in the woods, not responding to my calls, in hopes that I would leave without her. She could remain with her Benji. My dogs plan and execute plots as well as retain and appropriately recall information.

Every dog owner has observed the uncanny perception of canines. My dogs know when we are going to the country. It is unrelated to how I am dressed or what preparations I make before the trip. I have deliberately guarded against giving any behavioral or visual clues, and still they know. I can dress, follow the same routine, and leave without notice, but if I do the same and am going to the country, all the dogs gather eagerly at the door.

Dogs are more masterful than most human friends at judging one's mood. They respond appropriately to your joy and your sorrow. If you are happy, they are there to play and frolic. If you're tired, they are guarded but stay close to let you know they are near. If you are grieved, they are sympathetic, often nestling close to you or laying a head in your lap. My dogs read me well and respond with appropriate understanding.

My experience of canine understanding convinces me of

their emotional life. They grieve as humans do. If I'm absent for a short while, my dogs' appetites fade, and other signs of depression emerge. They grieve not only for themselves and their human companions, but they grieve for one another. When Ranger, a poodle of eighteen years, had to be put to rest, Caesar, his companion of many years, mourned his absence for months. Caesar showed disinterest in food, aloofness, and a lack of his typical zest.

Ranger's death gave me a deeper insight into the emotional perception of dogs. At the time, I had two poodles, Ranger and Caesar, and Lu, a Belgian shepherd. Their favorite treat was canned corned beef. Whenever a can was opened, there was excited jockeying for the treat. On the morning Ranger was to be put to sleep, I opened a can of corned beef as a farewell treat. As Ranger lay eating his treat, Caesar and Lu stood across the room watching sadly, never wanting or expecting a morsel. They knew this was Ranger's and Ranger's alone, his parting token.

My experience has convinced me that they have the capacity to reason, to understand, to sympathize—in fact, to share the whole range of human emotions. The human capacity for these faculties may be more sophisticated, even more profound. However, in the perception of the thoughts and feelings of others and in devotion and faithfulness, the canine capacity often seems superior.

There have been studies on the intelligence and behavior of animals with illustrations of their ability to form plans, manipulate symbols, plot mischief, express sentiment, and master sign language. All pet owners experience pets mastering vocabulary, whether it is simply "come," "sit," or more complex variations. They manage deception with evidence of having formed anticipated results. We have long been aware of their superior capacity for hearing and sense of smell. They have remarkable gifts: detection of explosives, drugs, cadavers, and even potential seizures. They evidence great skills as Seeing Eye guides. To me, it is clear they think and can think about what they know.

Current attention to the mystic of animals that discovers they are more than dumb brutes encourages animal enthusiasts who have long felt something special about God's creatures. These discoveries may come as no news to those who have known animals well, but they should come welcomed by any who don't yet know so well all creatures great and small.

Mary Agnes, my husky, reasons quite well. Moreover, she has a skill for subtle deception and manipulation. There is her favored chair in our den that sits beside a glass door into the garden; next to this door is a smaller door for the dogs. My cousin Ben was sitting in Agnes's chair. She came outside the glass door and scratched at the door to be admitted. Ben repeatedly pointed to the dog's door, saying, "Agnes, come in your door." She looked at the dog door and again scratched at the glass door. This exchange repeated itself over and over until Ben rose out of exasperation to open the door for her. As he rose, Agnes darted like a bullet through the dog door and into "her" chair. When Ben turned around, Agnes was comfortably resting with an air of total innocence in his former seat.

What makes one wonder about the superiority of Agnes's reasoning is that a few days later, we were in the same situation, with the same exchange in progress between Ben and Agnes. It continued a little longer than before, but ultimately she wore Ben down. Frustrated, he cautiously rose to open the door for her, declaring, "You're not going to fool me again." But she did! Exactly as before!

Hannah, another husky, is a television fan. She intently and regularly watches her favorite programs. Hannah knows when her programs are to come on, recognizes their theme music, and comes running from anywhere in the house to the television set on hearing the first bars of the theme. She knows programs that precede her favorites and when they are on will arrange herself before the set to await the start of "her" program.

Animals have the power to reason, to will, and to make and act on decisions with an awareness of consequences. They also experience a diverse range of emotions. The only qualification might be the extent of these qualities. Yet dimension cannot be a deciding factor concerning the faculties of the soul; otherwise there would arise problems with claiming a soul for undeveloped infants and mentally challenged persons.

My mixed pit bull is a schemer. When he wants my chair, he barks at the door to be let out, and, like Mary Agnes, as I rise to open it, he will dash to the chair. He also begins a furious barking, as if an intruder is near, to divert the other dogs from their dinner plates. His problem, he has barked wolf too long. The other dogs no longer fall prey to his scheme.

When one of my dogs makes a "mistake," all my dogs avoid the place as though any one of them might be blamed for doing something wrong. Yet only one of them can actually be guilty. If I correct one's behavior toward another dog, the corrected one knows he has done something wrong. Even before I make the correction, evidence already appears of the expectation of a reprimand.

In my experience, animals are aware when they have done wrong. They show remorse and guilt. They even seek forgiveness.

One might argue that such awareness is a product of training and conditioning by human masters. I think of Lu and Caesar foregoing insistence for their beloved canned beef because this time was Ranger's final treat. I remember seeing a cardinal keeping a roadside vigil by the corpse of his stricken mate, oblivious to the busy traffic flowing continuously a few feet away.

A parishioner told me of a bird striking her picture window and falling stunned to the ground. When she looked out the window, she saw the bird's mate attempting to revive the fallen bird.

Each incident reveals moral values not imposed. A far greater moral consciousness among animals, even genuine altruism, is evident in the deep devotion and faithfulness often demonstrated to their human companions, even when unmerited. They have long ago mastered the grace of forgiveness.

I had a parishioner whose parents lived a distance away and whom she visited frequently with her dog. On one such visit, during the journey her dog became obviously agitated and exceedingly restless. She assumed the dog had a need to relieve himself. As soon as possible, she pulled over the car, and they got out to take care of the presumed business. Immediately, the car's engine burst into flames and began consuming the auto. She is certain her dog saved their lives.

The extraordinary capacity of dogs for detection and prediction is well known for their wide use for the detector of explosives, drugs, cancer, and cadavers as well as for prediction of seizures and discerning the necessary details to be effective guide dogs for the blind.

Do animals have souls? The Hebrew word meaning either "living creature" or "living soul" is used of them in scripture. We are increasingly becoming more aware of the extent they evidence the faculties of the soul that theology delineates. If there is reason the question cannot be answered unequivocally in the affirmative, there is adequate reason it cannot emphatically be answered in the negative.

Quite unmistakably, as we have seen, animals are the objects of God's eternal love. According to the scriptural evidence, they indeed do have a place in heaven.

Now, the question of real import remains, how do we fulfill our ethical responsibility inherent in this fact?

Man's Responsibility

CHAPTER 5

Man's Responsibility

D isorder and corruption were introduced into creation by the disobedience of man. His rebellion against God's command brought curse to the created order:

> "Cursed is the ground for thy sake; in sorrow shalt thou eat of it all the days of thy life; thorns also and thistles shall it bring forth to thee." (Genesis 3:17–18)

The apostle Paul writes "the creature was made subject to vanity, not willingly, but by reason of him who has subjected the same in hope" (Romans 8:20). Man is responsible for the creatures' fallen state. The creatures are dependent upon man's reconciliation to God for their restoration. "For the earnest expectation of the creature waiteth for the manifestation of the sons of God" (Romans 8:19).

The creatures waiting to be "delivered from the bondage of corruption into the glorious liberty of the children of God" are thus described:

"For we know that the whole creation groaneth and travaileth in pain together until now." (Romans 8:21–22)

The term "travaileth" is one for the labor of child birth. Creation is waiting to be born anew.

From the will and act of man has come the state that necessitates redemption: "since by man came death ... as in Adam all die" (1 Corinthians 15:21, 22). As man was the agent of creation's fall, so man is the agent of creation's redemption. Therefore, the promise of and the invitation to God's redemption throughout the biblical revelation is addressed to the will and obedience of man. Man's response affects creation's fate.

Here is the measure of the significance of God's having made man "to dress and to keep" the garden of His creation (Genesis 2:15). Man's assignment at creation was to have dominion over the creation and all the creatures (Genesis 1:18). That dominion clearly encompassed their fate in Eden and now as clearly encompasses their fate in heaven.

Noah and Moses were instructed to gather the creatures for inclusion in their experiences of God's mighty acts of redemption, the ark and the Red Sea crossing. Likewise, in His commissioning of His disciples, Jesus gave similar instructions: "Go ye into al the world and preach the gospel to every creature" (Mark 16:15).

Preach the gospel to every creature. How might the responsibility be fulfilled? The thought of delivering sermons in field and forest to beast and fowl does not quite seem to be it, though Francis of Assisi did it. The "gospel" is the good news in Christ. The question is how might this good news be conveyed to creatures and creation?

Certainly, each one's personal response to this good news in Christ is the primary enabler for creation's restoration. As the apostle Paul put it, "For the earnest expectation of the creature waiteth for the manifestation of the sons of God" (Romans 8:19). Possibilities present themselves.

Jesus's final words to His disciples were: "Ye shall be witnesses unto me ... to the uttermost parts of the earth" (Acts 1:8). His meaning is that the world shall see him through these disciples. Earlier, He had said to them, "Ye are the light of the world" and "ye are the salt of the earth" (Matthew 5:13–14). The former meant that the world would see the truth through them. The latter meant that they were a preservative and a seasoning for the world.

In terms of this responsibility to creation, the first obligation is to make known to creation and the creatures how God feels about His world, that He loves the world and desires to restore it to its created goodness. The world is the Lord's now and forever!

Again, how is this done in a practical and nonverbal proclamation? There is one truth repeatedly reinforced in the New Testament about Jesus's expectation in any response to Him. Jesus enjoins actions that speak.

> "Not everyone that sayeth unto me, Lord, Lord ... but he that doeth the will of my Father" (Matthew 7:21)

> "Therefore whosoever heareth these sayings of mine and doeth them, I will liken him unto a wise man which built his house upon a rock" (Matthew 7:24)

> "He that hath my commandments and keepeth them, he it is that loveth me." (John 14:21)

There are actions by which we may preach the gospel to every creature. There is the seriousness with which we undertake the God-given duty "to dress and to keep" the creation. This entails a responsibility to preserve and care for the whole creation and all God's creatures. This is the first responsibility God gave man, and it has been continuously reiterated since man's initial failure.

The assumption of personal responsibility is basic for the protection of the environment, its cleanup, and its recovery from damage done. From the Bible's point of view, this has been the inherent responsibility of man from his creation.

Since the disruption of harmony among the creatures originated with man, man's obligation is to restore this God-given benefit to creation. God Himself will fulfill it perfectly in His new creation. Until then, we are witnesses of God's love and purpose to a fallen world. Among the possibilities, this necessitates action for the prevention of cruelty to animals and their needless exploitation for human indulgence. Since we acknowledge that animals have feeling or emotion, we have to take a careful look at how we treat them. Further, we must bear witness to God's concern for endangered species being lost to His creation.

More than defensive action on behalf of the creatures, there should be positive acts evidencing God's love of "the world." Animals do respond to loving kindness even as humans do. I have known animals who were so mistreated and abused by humans that they grew distrustful and hostile toward people. These same animals, when exposed to care and loving kindness, became "new creatures."

Ranger, a poodle rescued from an animal shelter after much obvious abuse by former owners, found protective hiding places in the house. He moved from place to place by slinking along the walls, never coming out into open spaces, not responding when called. He bit my hand the first time I reached toward him to pet him. After many months, he became an animal that never wanted to leave your side. He would crawl into your lap for a nap.

Response to kind treatment is more obvious with domesticated animals and more obscure for most of us with wild animals. Yet the experience of trainers and animal ecologists with gorillas, monkeys, dolphins, sea otters, and other creatures from the wild indicate positive response to favorable human treatment. My personal experience has only been with animals more accustomed to some human proximity: birds, squirrels, deer. However, as a college student, I worked one summer on an alligator farm in Florida and made friends with a boa constrictor and, particularly, an indigo snake who enjoyed afternoon naps with me. I never attempted to pet the alligators.

The potential for harmony among all creatures must exist if there is to be a day when the young child shall play upon the adder's hole or the lamb lie down with the wolf. It has always seemed to me some special grace prevailed among the passengers aboard Noah's ark as they floated upon those ancient waters.

There is restorative work to be done in our treatment of creatures if we are to be faithful to God's commission. As we increasingly encroach upon their natural habitats, we must as increasingly assume responsibility for the availability of their food and shelter. It is God's will that they be inhabitants of the earth, and God has given man the responsibility as their caretakers. We must ultimately answer to God for this stewardship.

Each of us must determine the specifics of our response to

this God-given responsibility for the creation. It is important for all of us, though, to realize that it is our God-given responsibility. We cannot neglect its obligation.

There are three kind ladies, living in the countryside with adequate acreage, who have found a mission in life to give a home to abused and stray animals. They give home to an array of dogs, cats, horses, goats, occasional birds, opossums, and a raccoon. They have had nearly fifty dogs at one time among their residents. It's a pleasure to visit their enclave and be greeted by a sea of wagging tails and happy faces accompanied by a chorus of excited barking.

Canine skill for greeting and welcoming has long been a noticeable feature. My dogs, after even short separations of less than an hour, greet my return with the joy of a father receiving a returning prodigal. Each dog has a special characteristic to his welcome. Hannah jumps up on you for a body hug. Tina wants to give one soft lick to the tip of your nose. Mary Agnes presents her head for a scratch behind the ears. Mama Sarah rolls onto her back for a stomach rub. The welcome ends only when each one has made his particular contribution to the ritual. This much is obvious: you were missed, and there is delight all around at your return.

Speaking in terms like obligation and responsibility makes our task seem a chore. It has been my experience that realizing our relationship to creation, and particularly to the creatures, has made awareness of life's beauty, wonder, and joy more full. Appreciation of my own life and of life in general has been enhanced. Thinking of the regard in which all things are held by their Creator and that all things share in His glory makes the appreciation of all things deeper. Oneness with life and creation gives new dimension to a sense of oneness with God. Everything is more precious; everything is appreciated. Among the kindest, most caring people I have known are those who, feeling a responsibility for creatures and creation, have sought to fulfill it.

There are moments when I sense a wonder about the world in which I live. A sparrow lights in my palm to nibble crumbs. A turtle, being rescued from the middle of the road, doesn't retreat into his shell for fear of me. On the beach, a seagull lights on my shoulder to rest and accompany me as I walk along. It is a foretaste of the coming peace and harmony. The wonder and beauty of being alive is unavoidable, as is the feeling that there is indeed something very good about the way God originally created the world. We find a serenity and peace within when we discover harmony with the world about us. Such was the original paradise.

There are organizations and causes committed to the care of creation and creatures with which one might get involved. The extent of that is a personal decision determined by opportunity and personal interests. The essential thing is that we become sensitive to the responsibility and recognize the obligation to all that God has created and given into our keeping.

There are some very simple possibilities. Jesus compared the beginning of the kingdom of God to a mustard seed that begins as the smallest of seeds and grows to become a tree in which sparrows nest. There are "the smallest of seeds" that we can plant for the creatures. Scattered bread crumbs on frozen ground, hot water on an icy bird bath can be messages of God's love to hungry, thirsty fowl.

An obligation to help injured animals on the roadside or to rescue turtles in the middle of thoroughfares has seemed a responsibility to me. When traveling alone through the countryside, my personal habit has been to pray for the creatures I see. For fowl, cattle, herds, and pets, I have prayed, "Lord, bless them and bring them to your new heaven and earth." For creatures too near busy traffic, I pray, "Lord, protect them." For some, I pray that they would know someone's love, and for all, I give thanks for their practical gifts and/or the gift of beauty to my life and to our world. When I see buzzards at work, I thank God for them who do a job none of us wants. There are grounds for gratitude for every living thing, though I must admit my enthusiasm is weakest for flies, fleas, and cockroaches. But I recognize this as my problem.

More important than the means we find for expression is the realization of our responsibility as God's stewards of His world. Thereby, we undertake our share as God's coworkers in His new creation. Even in ancient Israel, there was recognition of the moral obligation to animals: "A righteous man regardeth the life of his beasts" (Proverbs 12:10).

Is My Dog in Heaven?

Conclusion

We began our journey with the question, is my dog in heaven? We had and were aware of strong personal inclinations about an answer. Many close to animals felt an affirmative answer the only appropriate response. But there are doubters. We set out on this study in search of a more authoritative answer than mere opinion, no matter how well informed.

The Bible is our authority for our expectation of eternal life. If animals are included there, their assurance of heaven is as firm as ours. In our study, we examined every biblical prototype for salvation: their presence in Eden, creation's ideal model; their inclusion aboard the ark of Noah's time; Moses's request to include their herds in their exodus from Egypt and their inclusion in the exclusion of the fate of the Passover's angel of death; in the covenant of the Sinai law, their inclusion in the fifth commandment's Sabbath rest, the foretaste of heaven's shalom; the New Testament Gospel of Jesus Christ ("God was in Christ reconciling the world unto himself" [1 Corinthians 5:19]); the specific New Testament references to heaven (animals in the heavenly chorus celebrating redemption in John's vision of heaven [Revelation 5:13]). Redemption is of all creation.

What a wonder awaits us in the fulfillment of the Old

Testament vision of the coming glory of the Lord in which all creation is at peace (wolf and lamb lying together), man and creatures in a restored relationship (the young child playing on the hole of the asp), an end to the predatory state of the creatures (the lion shall eat straw like the cow). It is the peaceable kingdom in which war is no more. Swords are pruning hooks. Harmony is restored among the creatures and among men.

The seeds of conflict are no more. Greed, selfishness, jealousy are no more. Our driving force becomes how to love unconditionally. The destiny ahead is restoration of the original creation, the one God pronounced "very good." It is the new heaven and new earth coming down from God out of heaven in John's revelation (Revelation 21). Creation's true shalom is restored.

The real conclusion to our matter is: man is responsible by his rebellion in Eden for the corruption of creation and the pain and destruction endured by nature and the creatures. Man's redemption is the necessity for creation's restoration. "For the earnest expectation of the creature waiteth for the manifestation of the sons of God" (Romans 8:19). Creation is waiting on us.

It comes to this: we are compelled by Jesus's final command, "Preach the gospel to every creature" (Mark 16:15).

The challenge is how to preach to the creatures, how to show them the love of their Creator in a faithful stewardship of all God has given to our care. Quite honestly, it's our challenge to discover life's true joy. We need to be about our Father's business.

Welcome Home

Epilogue

The question with which we began: is my dog in heaven? The Bible's answer: yes, indeed!

But we have a responsibility.

I have a fantasy: As I enter the gates of heaven, I am greeted by Brownie leading the corps of all the animals I have known. The scene is excited barking, wagging tails, dancing and jumping, each jockeying for a personal touch. It is but a fantasy, but it is one of my most blissful moments from life on earth. Perhaps the fantasy may not be too farfetched.

References

The Holy Bible, Authorized King James Version.

The Living Bible (Wheaton, Illinois: Tyndale House Publishers, 1971).

John Calvin, *Institutes of the Christian Religion*, translated by John Allen (Philadelphia: Presbyterian Board of Christian Education, 1559).

Printed in the United States
By Bookmasters